Contents

My Pink Stilettos - Winter Edition

"

When people won't give you an opportunity, Create one!

Larita Rice-Barnes
#IWokeUpToPurpose

LIVING OUT LOUD

You can fulfill your wildest dreams. That's what I'm doing! I've decided to live out loud every day, every second, every minute. You know the old saying you get one life so you might as well live it to the fullest. In a healthy and responsible way that is. My Pink Stilettos was a vision that became a dream come true. A vision to bring women together from all across the world. We all have gifts, skills, talents and abilities. There is a tribe that has been assigned to us all. Your tribe knows your vibe and your vibe attracts your tribe. I want to speak into your life. There's absolutely NOTHING that you cannot do. You have divinely been given everything that you need to succeed. It lives on the inside of you. It is called dunamis power. It's supernatural. It enables you to run through troops and leap over walls. It aligns you with greatness and it attracts the people, places and things that will help you get to the next level. Living out loud will cause you to lose some friends. But guess what the ones that you gain will be the ones that you need. Living out loud will require you to walk away from fear. Fear is a thief and enemy to our destinies. Fear ain't our friend. It's like Aldi the stock up store. It has all of our blessings stored up. Fear sits in our board rooms and make decisions for us. Fear is that door that we allow to keep us from crossing over to the other side. I want to encourage you today to step out and live loud. No fear. No Excuses Just set your mind and do it. The world is waiting on you to show up and show out.

Editor In Chief
Dr. Larita Rice-Barnes

FOUNDER OF LOANI

Professor Caroline Makaka, President/CEO of LOANI-LADIES OF ALL NATIONS INTERNATIONAL.

- Global Goodwill Ambassador, Creator of We Are The Change World Movement, USA International Chairperson & Chaplain for The Global of International Alliance & People of Choice, Guest Professor at Royal American University, UN/UNESC UK Full Chairman
- World Peace Ambassador,
- Founded Worldwide Leaders Association, selected as Top Global Chairperson of the Year by the International Association of Top Professionals (IAOTP)
- Selected as one of the Top 100 influential humanitarians in the world
- World Peace Ambassador,
- Editor in Chief & Founder of Loani International Magazine

The International Association of Top Professionals (IAOTP) is an international boutique networking organization who handpicks the world's finest, most prestigious top professionals from different industries . She has also been selected as a top 100 influential humanitarian in the world by (WPF)

Professor Caroline Makaka is a woman of many talents and an expert in many industries.

A lady with a vision and a mission to shape the future of the world.
Her impressive repertoire of some of the roles that she holds are that she is the USA International Chairperson and People of Choice programs which covers the department for The Global of International Alliance Online School Programs for all new International students that apply to the program in the USA at **The Global of International Alliance**, she is a guest professor at the **Royal American University** .
She is the In**ternational Human Rights & Traffic Control Global Ambassador, UN/UNESC Full Chairman, Star of The world leader**, **Female Civility Ambassador, Patron at an orphanage school in Africa, International Advisor for International Youth Society, philanthropist , a community leader**, and advisory board member for several Global organizations, **Women & children rights activist, World Peace Ambassador, an honoree Member of IAOTP, She is Chief Operating Officer of She inspire Me, Chief Executive Officer for Women Changing The World, Diversity & Inclusion International Ambassador & Chief Advisor at Future Young Leadership program.**

While inclusion with the International Association of Top Professionals is an honor in itself, only a few members in each discipline are chosen for this distinction. These special honorees are distinguished based on their professional accomplishments, academic achievements, leadership abilities, longevity in the field, other affiliations and contributions to their communities.

With over a decade of professional experience as a philanthropist, advocate and entrepreneur, Professor Caroline has certainly proven herself as an influential professional and an expert within her field. She is a dynamic, results driven leader who has demonstrated success in every role which she has ever served.

Her areas of expertise encompass a wide range of skills such as Philanthropy, Global leadership, Non-Profit Leadership, Charities, International Project Management, Human Resources, Leadership and Individual Counselling, Equality & Diversity, Youth Empowerment and Recognition Awards.

Before beginning her venture as a prominent Global Chairperson, Professor Caroline attended the University of Northampton and received her Master's degree in International and Global studies. She also earned her Doctorate degree and is trained in Global Leadership.

Currently, Professor Caroline is the Founder/ CEO of Ladies of All Nations International (LOANI) located in the United Kingdom. Covering over 188 countries worldwide, LOANI's mission is to promote equality, diversity and inclusiveness regardless of age, race, gender, sexuality, religion, disability, etc. LOANI brings women together from various backgrounds, cultures, creeds, nationalities and races in an effort to alleviate difficulties and enhance development of their communities. They also highlight the importance of health and education to raise awareness against diseases and all kinds of abuse and celebrate and support each other through struggles and success.

Professor Caroline Makaka also created WE ARE THE CHANGE WORLD MOVEMENT to drive change, create dialogue & raise more public awareness.

During the pandemic We Are The Change World Movement brought together

Over 200 women & men from around the world.

They took action using their voices & actions to **MAKE CHANGE HAPPEN.**

In her own words, "As part of the change initiative, we are using our collective voices to motivate change as we come together in solidarity, supporting & encouraging each other, creating awareness and uniting for good causes"

Unite

LOANI also operates **Beautiful Survivors World of Honors,** which celebrates and honors survivors as heroines and empowers them to move out of the position of victims. They aid survivors to realize their true potential in life, it gives value and purpose for leading a more fulfilling life and taking pride in how far they have come.

As a Chairperson & founder for **Galaxy of Stars Young Inspirational Awards**, Professor Caroline lends her expertise through this movement. They recognize, honor, acknowledge, encourage and promote young people's talents, abilities and culture, building confidence, rewarding their efforts and creating a positive learning environment setting a high standard for to individual motivation and shaping the future leaders of tomorrow.

Throughout her illustrious career, Professor Caroline has received awards, accolades and has been recognized worldwide for her outstanding humanitarianism and leadership. Professor Caroline Makaka has been selected as one of the top **50 most inspirational black women in the United Kingdom** and received a special recognition for **Global Leadership of Humanity** for uplifting the underprivileged & empowering survivors. She was also selected as the Finalist for the **Female**

Civility Award & inducted in **The Global Library of Female Authors**. She is also part of the 2020 **Women of Inspiration by Universal Women Network in Canada.**

She has been named by **UN/UNESC** as one of the 100 volunteers who brighten the world by their commitment to the community

During the pandemic, Professor Makaka was selected as one of the recipients to receive a special recognition towards the contribution of the world development & raising awareness.
Some of the awards she has received in recognition of her work include, P**hilanthropy Award by Waterfront Awards in Canada, Global Peace Award by Global Academy for Human Excellency** in the Philippines, **Women of Excellence Award at the House of Parliament** in the UK , **100 Successful Visionary leaders** , **Inspiring Indian Women Special recognition Award** at The House of Parliament for supporting the Indian communities across the globe, **Dr. Sarvepalli Radhakrishnan Award** of Honor by Mentorx **Global Women Who Care Award** in Malaysia, **MTM special recognition Award, Leadership Recognition Award** from the the President of the Egyptian International Organization of Ambassadors for Peace

and Human Sciences, **World Star Award** from Yemen and a Medal in Excellency of leadership by Entity of Future Leaders in Egypt.

In recent years, Professor Caroline was honored twice with the **Women of Excellency Award** given by the Universal Peace Federation and the School of Beauty and Arts Mumbai in Delhi, India. She was awarded by **USA Global Chambers**, Florida, as one of the 100 Most Successful Women.

Professor Caroline received the **Women Appreciating Women Honoree Award**. She was granted the **Dr. Pauline Long Award** for her Humanitarianism. Professor Caroline was honored with the VIE Equality & Diversity Award (Chennai, India) as well as Female Role Model in Morocco & Goodwill Ambassador. She has won the International Achievers Award in the UK and the Panache Excellence Award for Community Support & also she has been awarded as part of the Global Iconic Women Creating a better world for all just to name a few.
Due to the contribution of her work globally, All Women Rock Global based in USA has created a Global Category in Honor of Professor Caroline Makaka.

Compassion

Every Year one person will receive a special Award named after her called

Professor Caroline Makaka Global Excellency & Achievement Award. This is in honor of her contribution to the society. She has also been selected as a recipient of Global dreams & making a change special award.

In addition to these notable merits, Professor Caroline has devoted a significant amount of her time and proficiency, serving the underprivileged. She is an active member within her community and throughout the world. Professor Caroline has volunteered, facilitated charity events and funded educational seminars and workshops to empower the impoverished specifically, in third world countries. She brings all people together in the hope to improve lives and strengthening society.

Looking back, Professor Caroline attributes her success to her benevolence, her compassion and her ability to embrace diversity. She remains passionate about all of her endeavors and loves collaborating with other professionals to create opportunities for those she serves. When not working, she enjoys traveling and spending time with her family. For the future, Professor Caroline will continue uniting cultures, serving communities, loving and uplifting the most vulnerable, supporting and helping as many people as she can to create positive changes for the greater good.

GLOBAL IMPACT LEADERSHIP ALLIANCE

OUR VISION

Our vision is to support and connect developing countries through economic development, advocacy through legislation, fund development, and spiritual growth. with a focus on enhancement through our innovative ideas we will increase economic development through the import and export of goods and services.

KEY AREAS

GILA has strategically identified key leaders from across the globe who are skilled in their crafts and have a passion to lead, train and develop world-class leaders. Our focus is to dominate the 7 areas of influence, which are:

BUSINESS | ARTS & ENTERTAINMENT | MEDIA | GOVERNMENT | FAMILY | EDUCATION | RELIGION

www.globalimpactnow.org
media@globalimpactnow.org

ARTS

&

ENTERTAINMENT

Soulfully Music

By: Shawna Dominique Harris

Music. It pulls you into a moment in time where just a memory of where you were or what you were doing when you first heard that one verse or voice makes you want to hold on and groove forever. While I didn't know that music would become such an integral part of my life, I knew at a young age that I too had been pulled in.

I was wrapped into the harmonies and things that a singer could do with their voice and I loved lyrics and poetry.

Around age 7, I realized I could mimic some of my favorite singers and that I didn't sound too bad doing it. Although I was extremely shy and cried through every church solo I was given, I was so enthused by music and singing. Fast-forward to high school, I was being raised by my great-grandparents who pastored a church, Gospel Lighthouse Apostolic Temple, with a small congregation. My God-sisters and I eventually would become the choir and musicians. This is where I would say I began to hone my skills, find my voice and build the foundation of my musical career. It was also at this time that I gave my life to Christ and knew that gospel music was the genre for me. The songs not only moved me and helped me through some of the through times of my life, but they also did the same for others a round me. Starting out as a kid who just wanted to sing, I honestly had no idea that I would be afforded opportunities to share the stage with singers I admire (Pastor John P. Kee, Tasha Cobbs Leonard, J.J. Hairston, Byron Cage, Marvin Sapp, to name a few).

I've been afforded the opportunity to travel the world, release an album (2014, God Is Able) and meet and sing for Pope Francis (2019). I never even imagined that I would be given the privilege to sum up my musical journey in a few short words. The scripture "Delight yourself in the Lord and He will give you the desires of your heart" (Psalm 37:4) is the one I would use to best describe my musical journey thus far. Like everyone, I've stopped, I've started, I've overcome obstacles unimaginable to me but the love I have for the Lord and the desire to share the love he gives through the gift I've been given is where my passion really lies. That's what keeps me going. The events, the stages, the people I meet along the way, the assignments, the opportunities, the music I create; those are just the benefits of the journey. So, at 35, I don't cry through my solo's anymore because I'm afraid. I mostly cry because I'm grateful. I'm grateful that music pulled me in.

"

You Can NEVER Cross The River Standing At The Bank.

Larita Rice-Barnes
#IWokeUpToPurpose

BEAUTY

&

BRAINS

Fredrina Walker

Granite City, IL

Married 17 years, Mother & G-momma of 6. A Teacher, Disciple of Jesus.

A Cosmetologist, & Mary Kay Beauty Consultant 26 yrs.

Wellness Promoter with Melaleuca. Aspiring fitness trainer.

"My Passion is to help people pursue total Body Health & Wellness!"

www.marykay.com/fdrina
www.salonsatreice.com
www.melaleuca.com/fredrinawalker

Skin-Care regiment before makeup application

It's important that you start with a Clean Canvas. Here are the 5 Most Important Things your skin needs to be Clean, Healthy, Fresh, Hydrated & Glowing

1. A Cleanser-deep clean dirt and oil away
2. A Mask/Exfoliating-remove dead skin cells for smooth skin
3. Toner-to freshen skin and close pores
4. Moisturizer-to hydrate and moisturize
5. Protect-sunscreen, primer, foundation

Depending on your skincare needs, you would use products that are for your skin type. Whether Dry/Normal, Combination/Oily, Sensitive, or Acne prone, there is a product line for you. Now I recommend the best skincare since sliced bread and ice cream, which are Mary Kay Skincare lines of course.

Side note: There is one for the whole family. Men, Women and teens.
I have used MK products since I was 19. I suffered with Eczema, my whole life, on my face and body. I've found Mary Kay Products to work wonderfully for me.

Be sure that whatever you choose, gives you the 5 Most Important Things to have a Refreshed, Hydrated, Smooth Canvas.

Once you complete your skincare, then you can begin applying your foundation and glamour to create a look that reflects a Beautiful You. NEW YEAR! NEW YOU!!

If you would like a virtual appointment to learn more about how to take care of your skin, glamour tips or even learn a little about what I do, be sure to visit my Website and send me a message.

Happy Healthy Skin!!

Canesha Henry

CJH Brand

If you're natural and in this case meaning no relaxers, you've probably become a researcher, scientist, stylist and chemist by now! We are in the age of influencers, and vloggers and there's content being created everywhere to tell you everything you should be doing with your hair. You've probably read that you should only use sulfate-free shampoo. Let me just tell you why this is a BIG no in my salon. Sulfate is a cleansing agent that is used to deeply clarify the scalp and unclog cuticles. Sure, after shampooing your hair it'll feel much dryer, but that's because you've stripped your hair of buildup and debris. To add natural oils and vitamins in your hair you should always follow up with a conditioner. Your shampoo and conditioning process is way more important than any other product you can buy. This is oftentimes what everyone is less likely to invest in. This can help prevent excessive shedding, breakage and dryness. Sulfate-free shampoo should not be your main shampoo.

BONUS TIP: Shampoo with warm water and rinse your conditioner with cool water*

BIO:
In 4 short years she's worked on play and movie sets, with your favorite artists, and TV and radio personalities. She helps to cultivate and monetize skills by way of coaching and counseling. She's known for her creative ideas, faith and wisdom. CJ passionately works to improve brands professionally and personally to attract the money you want to make.

info@cjhbrand.com

www.cjhbrand.com

FB @cjhbrand

IG @cjhbrand

FALL EDITION

MY PINK STILETTOS

2020

Living Out Loud

Women Empowerment

I Survived Breast Cancer

DR. MISSY JOHNSON

Dr. Larita Rice-Barnes

WOMEN

&

POLITICS

Honors and Awards

- Tanda Canon Foundation Ministries Service Award -03/2018
- GILA -Global Impact Trail Blazer Award 4/2019
- The Blessing of Africa Champion of Change Award 6/2019
- The Royal Theatre Celebration Global Powerful Vision Award 9/2019
- GEM- USA Global Empowerment Movement

Women as Political Leaders

Atlanta, Georgia

I Ambassador Dr. Lenora Peterson Maclin Ph.D.

I have had the opportunity to volunteer and campaign for some awesome phenomenal candidates in my life.

I first took interest in politics back in the sixties around the age of 10. My first job was stuffing envelopes for a city Councilman whose name was Virgil Brown. He was elected back in the year of 1967 as a Councilman in the Glenville community in my hometown Cleveland, OH.

I also became very active under Rep. Stephanie Tubbs Jones who was an American politician who served as the U.S. Representative for Ohio's 11th congressional district from 1999 until her death in 2008. She also developed a community congressional committee to help better our black community outreach in neighborhoods in Cleveland Ohio eastside. I was a member of a community congressional committee for 3 years in the early 2000's.

I always loved being a part and a member of an U.S. political party. I served as a Democratic committee member for female candidates such as Democrat Hillary Clinton. She made history as a woman leading candidate for the presidential election in 2016.
I also served as a volunteer for Stacey Yvonne Abrams campaign. An activist and author who served in the Georgia House of Representatives. Stacey Abrams became the first black woman to gain a major U.S. party nomination for governor of Georgia. Abrams ran for governor of Georgia in 2018 for the Democratic primary.

There will always be and still are some very powerful women in politics like these awesome women. Here are a few more. Ohio Congresswoman Marcia Fudge- Served 2008-Present, Maxine Waters Democrat – California Served: 1991 – Present, Barbara Jordan Democrat – Texas Served: 1973 - 1979

WOMEN AS POLITICAL LEADERS

Harvard Kennedy School wrote to CNN that: In the next 100 years, women may dominate US politics.

When it comes to women and power in America, 2020 is a landmark, but also a question. We are marking the centennial of the ratification of the 19th Amendment enfranchising women even as we ask: Whose votes -- and stories -- are left out of the narrative? What of the work toward equity that has yet to be done?

We are seeing Sen. Kamala Harris take the stage as a vice presidential candidate: the first Black woman, the first South Asian woman, on a major party ticket. But we are also asking: What will it take for a woman to become President of the United States? In 1917, members of the National Woman's Party picketed the White House, carrying banners that included the question: "Mr. President, How Long Must Women Wait for Liberty?" In 2020, players in the Women's National Basketball Association are competing in a bubble without fans but in front of the world wearing jerseys bearing the name of Breonna Taylor.

How far have we come since 1920? What did it mean to be an ally then, and what does it mean now? What are the most important political questions confronting women today who seek equity, who strive for justice, who want to step into their power?

Goodwill Ambassador Dr. Lenora Peterson-Maclin PhD

Obtained her Doctoral degree in Philosophy Theology studies on April 19, 2013 from Luther Rice College & Seminary and The Sure Foundation Theological institute Dr. Peterson earned a Doctorate Degree of Theology in the Keys, Governing Laws and Principle. She holds a certification from **Harvard X online program in Humanitarian Response to Conflict and Disaster.**

She is a Licensed International Chaplain Minister. She is the founder of Vision in You Outreach Foundation Inc. in Duluth, GA since 2006. The new GIA chaplaincy online school program.

Dr. Peterson is presently the official Global Goodwill Ambassador Chief Executive Director for **Global International Alliance Program Corporation for National Volunteer Community Service Online, Honorary Advocate Leadership & People of Choice Program** of Uniting in Humanitarianism Non-Profit Organization Program a 501c3. The Global of International Alliance Online School was established in 2016 and is an accredited program under IACET Standards for Lifelong Learning.

Dr. Lenora Peterson-Maclin is a published author of the newly released book, **The Lady, The Level, The Loyalist** (3/2020)

She graced the front cover of The LOANI Magazine October 2020 Issues out of UK. She now the United States of American Chairperson for "Ladies of all Nations International (LOANI) This a group that is connected with women from all around the world spanning over 100 countries. LOANI headquarter is located in London, UK. **Ladies of All Nations Movement** is an organization who we have partnered with. There are many women from all around the world that advocates for change.
Aaron's Beard School of the Prophet's Bible

College – 05/11/2018
Member of International Congress of Churches & Ministries Marketing Management in Church business for over 700,000 members at more than 200 local chapters 3/09/2014

Endorsement and Awards

- City of Chicago, IL: Mayor Lori E Lightfoot Office/ Recognition of Honor for my work with Global Empowerment Movement as an advocate for Human Trafficking in Africa 4/4/2020
- City of New York City Council Citation: to Incorporation of National Community Service 1st Annual Inner City Gun Violence Award Service - June 16, 2018

- Proclamation: For outstanding work anti-gun violence in community service-September 22, 2018
- The City of Chicago: Recognition of Honor from six different departments in the State of Illinois for The Advocate Community service program- April 5, 2019
- New York, NY: UN Women 220 East 42nd Street: United Nations Economic and Social Council (ECOSOC) - January 23, 2019.
- Atlanta, GA: Congressional District Congressman John Lewis: Certificate of Special Congressional Recognition from U.S. Representative for Georgia's 5Th district-October 19, 2017

Resolution - Senator Donzella James 8/2019
Senator Tonya P Anderson /06/2019
The State of Georgia Outstanding Citizen as a Goodwill Ambassador 11/2016

Memberships

- International Association of Women IAW Regional Networking 10/2020
- International Association for Continuing Education and Training Accreditation (IACET)
- National Committees for UN Women are independent non-governmental organization Member of New York 6/2019
- Embassy Consulate General New York city, Advocate Member NCNW National Council of Negro Women Inc.
  633 Pennsylvania, Ave, NW Washington, DC 20004 - 6 1/2020

MEN

SUPPORTING

WOMEN'S

LEADERSHIP

Juard M. Barnes

Indianapolis, Indiana

Living in a time where the leadership of women is accelerating is exciting.

Having more women in leadership is a powerful and immensely important development. It's important because female leadership changes the perceived conception about who can lead and what qualities are necessary to have in leadership positions.

The recent election of a presidential ticket that included a woman, a Black woman as vice president of the most powerful country on earth is world changing.

Women in these types of roles break down barriers and show everyone what women can - and should - achieve.

What are the roles men could and should play in these transformative times? Recent studies show that the public sees little distinction between men and women relative to many leadership traits. Large majorities say that when it comes to intelligence and innovation, men and women display those qualities equally. And solid majorities see no gender differences in ambition, honesty and decisiveness.

Unfortunately, even given all of this evidence, powerful women tend to be judged in different ways than powerful men. The goal of this brief piece has nothing to do with tackling that age old truth. I'm much more committed to lending a voice to the importance of men, particularly men who are powerful in their own right, to act as thought partners to their female counterparts. It's always tempting to use the word 'empower' in these instances.

However, a quick look at synonyms for the word "empower", and it becomes immediately apparent that another word or phrase is warranted. Empower suggests concepts like authorizing, enabling, warranting... You get the picture. I prefer to see the relationship between men and women in professional settings as symbiotic. An opportunity for sharing powerful, world changing ideas.

There is much to be gained by everyone when there is mutual respect and active support by men for their women counterparts.

Men who (walk in partnership) with the life success of women often find that they have increased access to information and broader networks in their own organization, especially if they (walk with) someone outside their functional business unit, says David Smith, co-author of Athena Rising: How and Why Men Should Mentor (again, I don't personally love the word mentor) Women (Bibliomotion, 2016).

The Harvard Business School found that some of the key behavioral themes associated with gender inclusive leadership that support women's career advancement are:

- *using their authority to push workplace culture toward gender equality*
- *thinking of gender inclusiveness as part of effective talent management*
- *providing gender-aware mentoring and coaching*
- *practicing other-focused leadership, not self-focused leadership*

The public and transparent execution of a truly cooperative relationship fully supported by men is one of the powerful opportunities for this generation. I want to be counted among a growing number of men who walk in unity with the powerful leadership of women around the world!

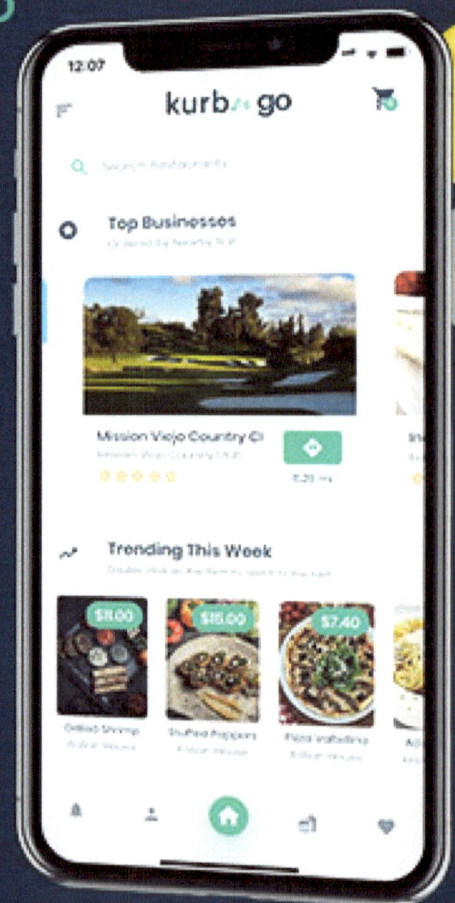

WOMEN

EMPOWERMENT

&

AUTHOR'S

SPOTLIGHT

Women Empowerment

Coach Stacy Bryant

Emotionally Intelligent Leadership

Emotional intelligence may be a new term for you – but you may be hearing it more often when the traits of leadership are discussed. Emotional intelligence has been found to be an important factor in leadership abilities. More and more, organizations are seeking to recruit those who display a strong leaning toward emotional intelligence.

Employees experience more job satisfaction, retain more information and display better performances when led by emotionally intelligent leaders. But what is emotionally intelligent leadership? Basically, it's certain factors which leaders have that make them stand out and perform better than the rest, including:

- **Recognition of emotions in others** - Emotionally intelligent leaders are aware of other's moods and feelings in the work environment. They're tuned in, emotionally, to their employees.

- **Emotions of others don't affect them personally** - Employees who express anger or are judgmental sometimes let their emotions get away from them. The emotionally intelligent leader doesn't take such emotions personally.

- **Remain calm in challenging situations** - Expressing yourself in emotionally charged situations can be damaging to others around you. It's best to keep them to yourself and later address the problem or situation in a calm and reassuring way.

- **Ability to put yourself in another's position** - Trying to understand the other person's point of view when it differs from your own is sometimes difficult, but the emotionally intelligent leader can look at a situation from another's perspective and gain more knowledge of how to address the problem.

- **Ability to regulate himself** - A leader also leads himself and is able to regulate his or her feelings and emotions in a positive manner. He strives for a healthy lifestyle and is always learning.

- **Motivates others** - Motivating others through positivity is another quality of the emotionally intelligent leader. When a person leads through threats and intimidation, nothing productive can occur. It may seem like you're progressing and meeting goals, but if it isn't handled in a positive way it will be like a structure built on sand.

To become an effective, emotionally intelligent leader, you must develop a true understanding about how people are affected by their emotions and the actions and decisions of others. Working with your subordinates rather than dictating the job to them is the difference between being successful – or failing at your leadership responsibilities.

Working on key areas of emotional intelligence can help you excel in all areas of leadership and ensure success in your future endeavors.

Authors Spotlight

Stacee Ferguson

Hi there! My name is Stacee Ferguson! I'm 36 years old and an entrepreneur. I have four children ranging in age from 8 years old to 16 years old. I am the founder and CEO of My Coffee Talk LLC. My Coffee Talk is a blog I started to bring enlightenment, encouragement and inspiration to the world. I'm also a brand ambassador for a health and wellness company and a licensed Life & Health Insurance agent. I'm licensed in MO & TX.

I have worked hard since I was a teen. I was born and raised in St. Louis, MO. Children were never a part of my plan, but playing baby mama wasn't either, so I married young. Needless to say I wasn't ready for what came next. I went through so much during my childhood and in my marriage, I feel like I can overcome anything! I share a bit of my struggles and triumphs in my newly released book "I Am Redeemed, A Wretch Undone". My book can be found on Amazon, Google Play and my website **https://mycoffeetalkblog**.com.

Authors Spotlight

Alisha Thorpe

Alisha Thorpe is a retired nurse, counselor and ordained Evangelist who believes in sharing the word of God and healing lives through the power of her testimony. The daughter of Pentecostal parents, she was called by God at an early age to minister to his people. Evangelist Thorpe resides in Belleville, IL where she continues to be active in her local ministry, Love Church, and outreach ministries.